PREDATOR VS. PREY

Owl vs. Mouse

Mary Meinking

Raintree

Chicago Illinois

www.heinemannraintree.com

Visit our website to find out more information about Heinemann-Raintree books.

To order:

☎ Phone 888-454-2279

💻 Visit www.heinemannraintree.com to browse our catalog and order online.

Edited by Rebecca Rissman, Dan Nunn,
    and Catherine Veitch
Designed by Joanna Hinton Malivoire
Levelling by Jeanne Clidas
Picture research by Hannah Taylor
Production by Victoria Fitzgerald
Originated by Capstone Global Library
Printed and bound in China by CTPS

14 13 12 11 10
10 9 8 7 6 5 4 3 2 1

Library of Congress Cataloging-in-Publication Data

Meinking, Mary.
  Owl vs. mouse / Mary Meinking.
    p. cm.—(Predator vs. prey)
  Includes bibliographical references and index.
  ISBN 978-1-4109-3936-4 (hc)
  ISBN 978-1-4109-3945-6 (pb)
1. Owls—Food—Juvenile literature. 2. Mice—Defenses—Juvenile literature. 3. Mice—Preditors of—Juvenile literature. 4. Predation (Biology)—Juvenile literature. I. Title. II. Title: Owl versus mouse.
  QL696.S83.M445 2011
  598.9'7153—dc22   2010016925

Acknowledgments

We would like to thank the following for permission to reproduce photographs: Alamy Images pp. 10 (© mammalpix), 20 (© Don Vail); FLPA pp. 5 (Gary K Smith), 15 (S Charlie Brown), 17 (Simon Litten), 19 (David Hosking), 26 (Erica Olsen), 28 (Gary K Smith); istockphoto pp. 6 (© S. Cooper Digital), 9 (© Jason Crader); naturepl.com pp. 8 (Mike Read), 24 (Rolf Nussbaumer); Photolibrary pp. 7 (Oxford Scientific/ Robin Redfern), 12 (age fotostock/ Dan Leffel), 18 (Oxford Scientific/ Tony Tilford), 21 (Juniors Bildarchiv), 22 (Rolf Nussbaumer); Photoshot pp. 4 (Woodfall), 13 (NHPA/ Ernie Janes), 14 (NHPA/ Stephen Dalton), 16 (NHPA/ Stephen Dalton), 23 (Imagebrokers), 25 (Imagebrokers), 29 (NHPA/ Jordi Bas Casas); shutterstock pp. 11 (© Alexey Stiop), 27 (© Dr Morley Read).

Cover photographs of a barn owl reproduced with permission of Photolibrary (Peter Arnold Images/ Gerard Lacz), and a field vole reproduced with permission of Photolibrary (Oxford Scientific/ Mark Hamblin).

We would like to thank Michael Bright for his invaluable help in the preparation of this book.

Some words are shown in bold, **like this**. You can find out what they mean by looking in the glossary.

Content

Talons Vs. Tails

Claws scratch! Teeth gnaw! Two animals meet nose-to-beak in the grassy battlefield. Here's a silent hunter, the barn owl. It's up against a scampering challenger, the mouse.

mouse

owl

These animals live in fields across Europe. Both have strengths that will help them in this battle.

PREDATOR
barn owl

LENGTH: 1 1/2 feet

WEIGHT: 1 pound

TOES PER FOOT: 4

Key
 where these types of barn owls and mice live

PREY
mouse

LENGTH: 6 inches

WEIGHT: 2 ounces

TOES PER FOOT: 4 on front feet and 5 on back

Europe

Flying Mouse Trap

The barn owl is an excellent hunter. It uses its sharp claws, or **talons**, to catch and kill **prey**.

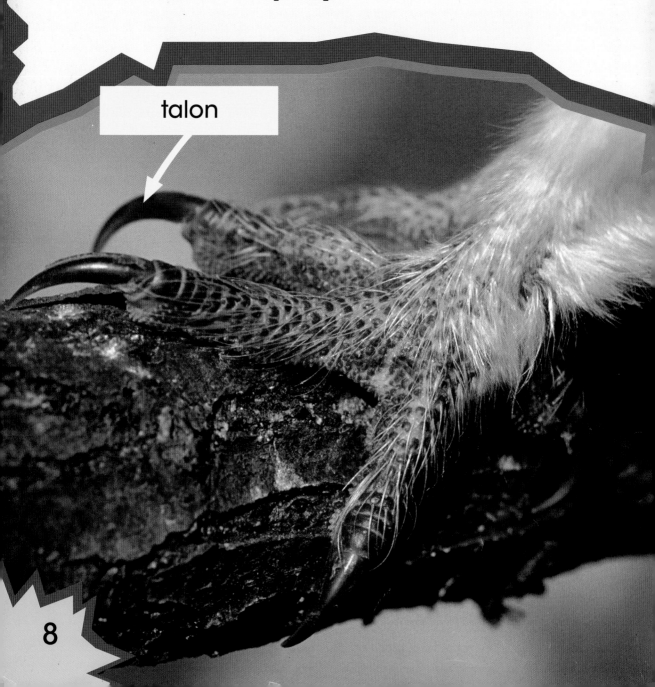

talon

Did You Know?

Barn owls' ears are hidden under their feathers. One ear is higher than the other. This helps the owl learn where a sound is coming from. They use their hearing to find prey in the dark.

Fast Mice

If danger is near, the mouse darts under cover or back to its nest. It can run at eight miles per hour. But can it run faster than an owl flies?

Did You KNOW?

Mice chew paths that are one to two inches wide through the grass. Mice use these hidden paths to move around without being seen.

Who's Hungry?

The barn owl is a **carnivore**, or meat eater. It must eat one and a half times its weight in food every night. The mouse eats grass, plants, and tree bark. It eats over half its weight in food each day.

Did You Know?
The mouse stores some food underground to eat in the winter.

13

Night Shift

At sunset the mouse crawls out of its grassy nest. The owl wakes up from its nap. It climbs out of the hole in the tree where it hid all day. The owl hasn't eaten since last night. And it's hungry!

The mouse finds a seed to eat. It sits on its back legs and holds the food with its front paws. The owl sits on its **perch,** or resting place listening for anything moving. It hears something. Is it a mouse?

Did You Know?
The owl's hearing is so good that it can hear a mouse under plants or snow.

The owl flies off its **perch**. It **glides** with its feet tucked back. It flies low and slowly towards the sound. It hears the animal hundreds of meters away.

Did You Know?

Owls' feathers have a fuzzy front edge. This **muffles,** or silences, the sound of their wings beating. This lets owls quietly sneak up on **prey**.

The mouse freezes. It sees something moving. The mouse stamps its hind foot, like a rabbit, to warn other mice. It runs towards its nest. The owl's wings open all the way out to slow down. Its tail feathers work like a brake to stop it.

Did You Know?

An owl's wings can be three feet across. That's as long as eight mice in a line.

The owl's feet swing forwards with its sharp **talons** out. Even though it can't see the mouse, the owl hears it running. The owl snatches the running mouse with its talons.

mouse

The mouse tries to get free. It squeaks out a call for help. It wiggles and bites at the owl's feet. But it's trapped in the owl's strong **talons**. The owl grabs the mouse with its hooked beak. It takes off with its prize.

And the Winner Is...

...the owl! It returns to its **perch**. It gulps down the mouse, head first, without chewing.

Did You Know?

Owls swallow their food whole. The fur, bones, teeth, and feathers collect in their stomachs. There it's made into balls called **pellets**. The owl soon coughs up and spits out the pellets.

pellet

27

What Are the Odds?

The barn owl catches nine out of every 10 animals it goes after. As well as mice it eats birds, rabbits, frogs, and other animals. It eats four to eight creatures every night. That's over 1,400 animals every year!

bird

Glossary

carnivore animal that eats meat

glide move slowly and smoothly

muffle silence the sound of something

pellet ball of bones and feathers that is spat out by birds of prey

perch place for a bird to sit

predator animal that hunts other animals

prey animal that is hunted by other animals for food

talons sharp claws on a bird of prey

Find Out More

Books

Waters, Jo. *The Wild Side of Pet Mice and Rats.* Chicago: Raintree, 2005.

Whitehouse, Patricia. *Barn Owls.* Chicago: Heinemann Library, 2009.

Wojahn, Rebecca Hogue and Donald Wojahn. *A Temperate Forest Food Chain: A Who-Eats-What Adventure in North America.* Minneapolis, MN: Lerner Publications, 2009.

Websites

http://www.audubon.org/educate/kids/
Watch barn owls in their natural habitat on the National Audubon Society Website.

http://www.nwf.org/kids.aspx
Find out about the wild animals that live near you.

Index